VOICES OF ANCIENT EGYPT

BY KAY WINTERS

ILLUSTRATED BY

BARRY MOSER

LIBRARY
FRANKLIN PIERCE COLLEGE
RINDGE, NH 03461

NATIONAL GEOGRAPHIC

WASHINGTON, D. C.

To Marta Felber, who introduced me to Egypt —KW

For Kay —BM

The author, illustrator, and publisher would like to thank
Edward Bleiberg, Associate Curator, Egyptian, Classical,
and Ancient Middle Eastern Art, Brooklyn Museum of Art,
for carefully reviewing both text and illustrations for historical
accuracy and for supplying us with the proper
hieroglyphics for the titles.

Text copyright © 2003 Kay Winters
Illustrations copyright © 2003 Barry Moser

Published by the National Geographic Society.
All rights reserved. Reproduction of the whole or any part of the contents
without written permission from the National Geographic Society is strictly prohibited.

The illustrations in this book are watercolor on paper.
Book design by Bea Jackson.
The text of the book is set in Gilgamesh.

Library of Congress Cataloging-in-Publication Data

Winters, Kay.
Echoes of ancient Egypt / by Kay Winters ; illustrated by Barry Moser.
    p. cm.
Summary: Individual craftsmen, artists, and laborers describe the work
that they do in Egypt during the time of the Old Kingdom, and the
historical note places them in context.
ISBN 0-7922-7560-8 (hard cover)
1. Egypt—Civilization—To 332 B.C.—Juvenile literature. 2.
Occupations—Egypt—Juvenile literature. [1. Egypt—Civilization—To 332
B.C. 2. Occupations—Egypt.] I. Moser, Barry, ill. II. Title.
DT61 .W58 2003
932—dc21

                    2001007356

One of the world's largest nonprofit scientific and educational organizations, the
National Geographic Society was founded in 1888 "for the increase and diffusion of
geographic knowledge." Fulfilling this mission, the Society educates and inspires mil-
lions every day through its magazines, books, television programs, videos, maps and
atlases, research grants, the National Geographic Bee, teacher workshops, and innova-
tive classroom materials. The Society is supported through membership dues, charitable
gifts, and income from the sale of its educational products. This support is vital to
National Geographic's mission to increase global understanding and promote conserva-
tion of our planet through exploration, research, and education.

Visit the Society's Web site at www.nationalgeographic.com.

NATIONAL GEOGRAPHIC SOCIETY
1145 17th Street N.W.
Washington, D.C. 20036-4688 U.S.A.
Visit the Society's Web site: www.nationalgeographic.com

PRINTED IN THE UNITED STATES OF AMERICA

CONTENTS

About the Hieroglyphics

The titles in this book are printed in two languages—English and ancient Egyptian (hieroglyphics). The ancient Egyptian translations come from the *Concise Dictionary of Middle Egyptian* by R. O. Faulkner.

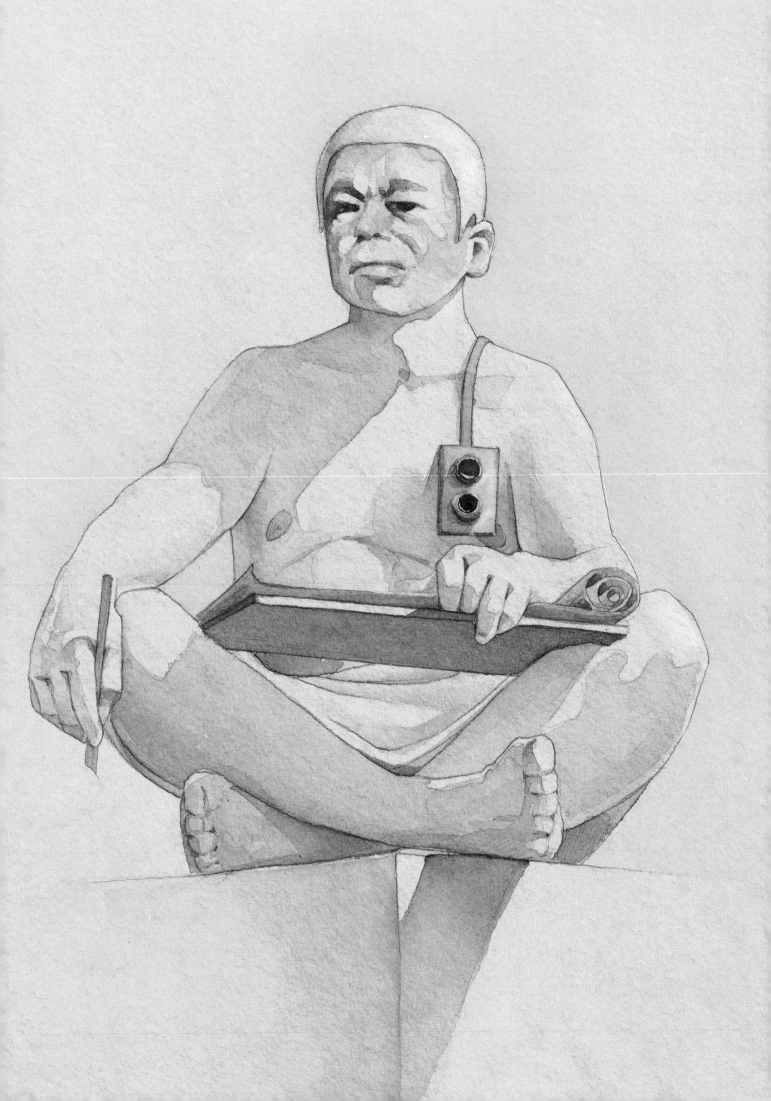

The Scribe

I study day and night,

learn law, literature, and mathematics,

copy retold tales.

I am my father's dream,

daring to be more than he.

While others bear lashes to build tombs,

dodge crocodiles to fish the Nile,

weave cloth in airless rooms,

I unlock secrets in ancient scrolls,

weave wisdom from times gone by.

In a kilt of white, I measure the Nile,

count the cattle, register the harvest.

No taxes on my goods!

Because of me, voices of the village come alive.

Hear my people speak.

With reed brush and cake of ink

I record our days.

The Farmer

My husband and I work the master's land.

After floods rise, we guide water into narrow lanes,

drenching dusty clay.

Weeks pass while water soaks the earth.

Time for the sowing of the seed.

The driver urges the oxen with a stick.

My husband pushes plough handles down deep.

The driver cries, "Pull hard." He prods the team.

I follow behind, breaking clods of soil

with my wooden hoe.

We scatter seed. Sheep trod and trample.

Seeds sink and settle into black mud.

Now is the time for waiting

for those first small shoots.

Now is the time for watching

for worms, mice, locusts, the hippopotamus.

All are enemies of the sower of seed.

At the harvest the scribe measures the grain.

The master is pleased.

We give thanks to the god Min, friend of the farmer.

We bow to barley, sing to the Nile.

Together we have worked the land.

The Pyramid Builder

The Nile is flooding. It's time!

Like thousands of my countrymen,

I leave my village and go to Giza to serve Pharaoh,

to carve his stairway to the sky.

I am a cutter of stone as well as a planter of seed.

Barges bring yellow limestone from dusty quarries.

Side by side with other stonecutters,

I lift my mallet, pound the chisel.

We size the stone, level the high spots,

square the two-ton block.

Haulers slide the stone on a sled.

Water bearers run ahead to soak the mud,

which coats the rising ramp.

Masons push the block into place.

A scribe keeps count.

Year after year, in sun that scalds, we toil for Pharaoh.

He gives us radishes, onions, bread to eat,

a place to sleep.

Each day I pray the gods will not let the stone I work

roll back and crush me into dust.

But I am proud to help shape the House of Eternity.

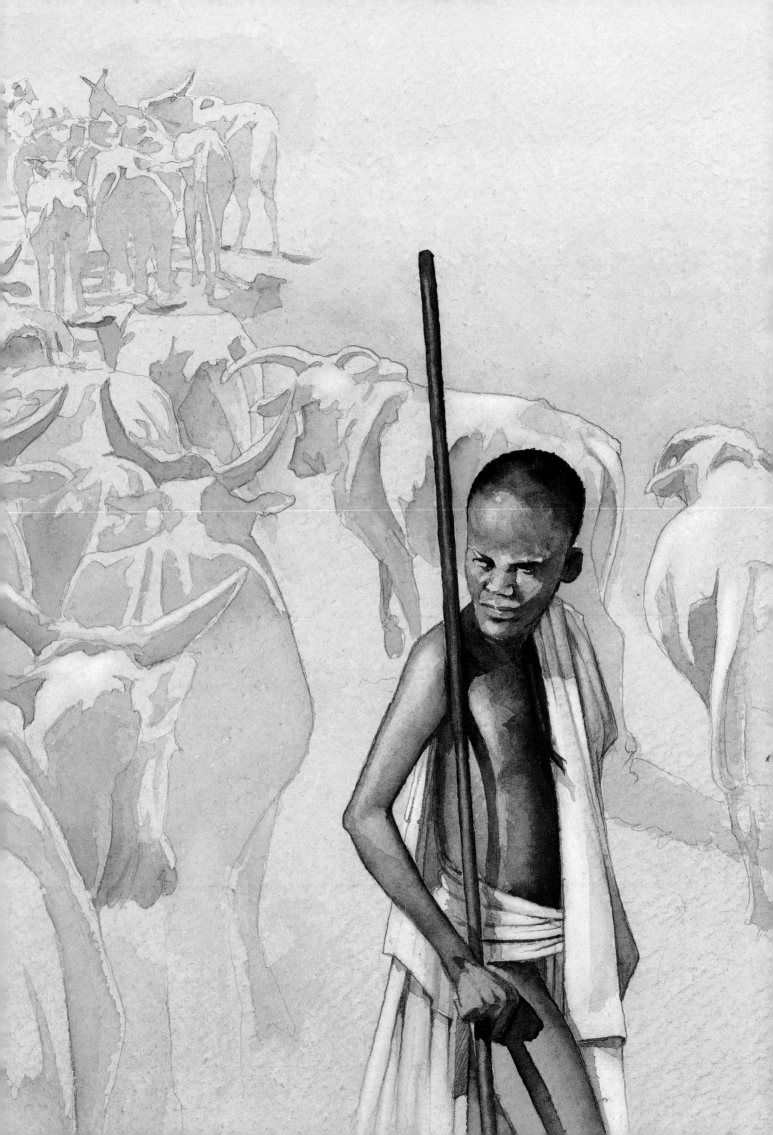

The Herdsman

The cattle are my children.

With soft words, I spend my days

tending, feeding, birthing.

I fatten cows with rolls from boiled dough.

In summer, we herdsmen travel north

where our cattle graze in grassy fields.

We live in reed huts, roast ducks upon the fire,

tell tall tales, and guard our herds.

Heading home, we wade the river's branch,

watchful for the crocodile.

I carry the smallest calf upon my back.

Now cattle, fat and sleek, await counting

by the scribe.

I am the herdsman,

the cows, my kin.

The Birdnetter

Look up! Look above!

The cranes, the doves, the ducks are coming.

I am the snarer of birds.

How fortunate I am to work in open air,

in green fields and leafy marshes.

Bright winged waterbirds, pigeons, and quail

swarm over Egypt.

My nets and traps are ready.

I trap geese then fatten them with dough,

just as the herdsman feeds his cattle.

Plump and tasty,

these birds could grace the Pharaoh's table

and sometimes do.

I water the crane, with his slim stilt neck,

a pretty present for the master's daughter.

My family and I do not go hungry,

for the sky is loud

with the beating of wings.

I am the birdnetter.

I wonder how it would feel

to fly?

The Washer of Clothes

I am a washer of clothes.

Brother to the crocodile,

I spend my days in water.

I soak the clothes, beat them with a wooden stave,

then wrap them around a stick

to wring out the wet.

White linen soils quickly in our hot dry land.

I scrub goose grease, wine stains, the juice of berries.

I deliver clean kilts, skirts, cloaks, and robes

to my master's household.

To be clean of body,

dressed in spotless garb

is the mark of those I serve.

The Nile is my workplace.

I know no other.

The Weaver

Weaving is women's work.

Ancient tales tell that goddesses

spun and wove the clothes of Osiris.

I follow in their sandal prints,

making linen smooth as silk.

The flax is boiled, beaten with hammers,

cleaned by hand.

The spinner chooses fibers to form her thread,

then twists and turns her spindles.

I work the warp and woof with the shuttle

on a horizontal loom.

Though days are long and the room is close,

my cloth shimmers in the sunlight.

It is packed unfolded into boxes

and carried off on poles

to the royal House of Silver.

My own garments may be coarse,

my husband just a peasant,

but I create cloth fit for gods.

The Goldsmith

My gold comes from Nubia,

where captives live in stone huts

and mine the vein.

I know the secret ways of working gold,

how to twist wires, cut strips, set stones.

I make jewelry for the living and the dead.

My circlets gleamed

on the arm of the Queen

as she rode down the Nile.

When she passed on

to the Land That Loves Silence,

those bracelets were tucked in her tomb.

I am the goldsmith.

My work glitters almost as bright as our sun god Re.

Village heads turn when I walk by.

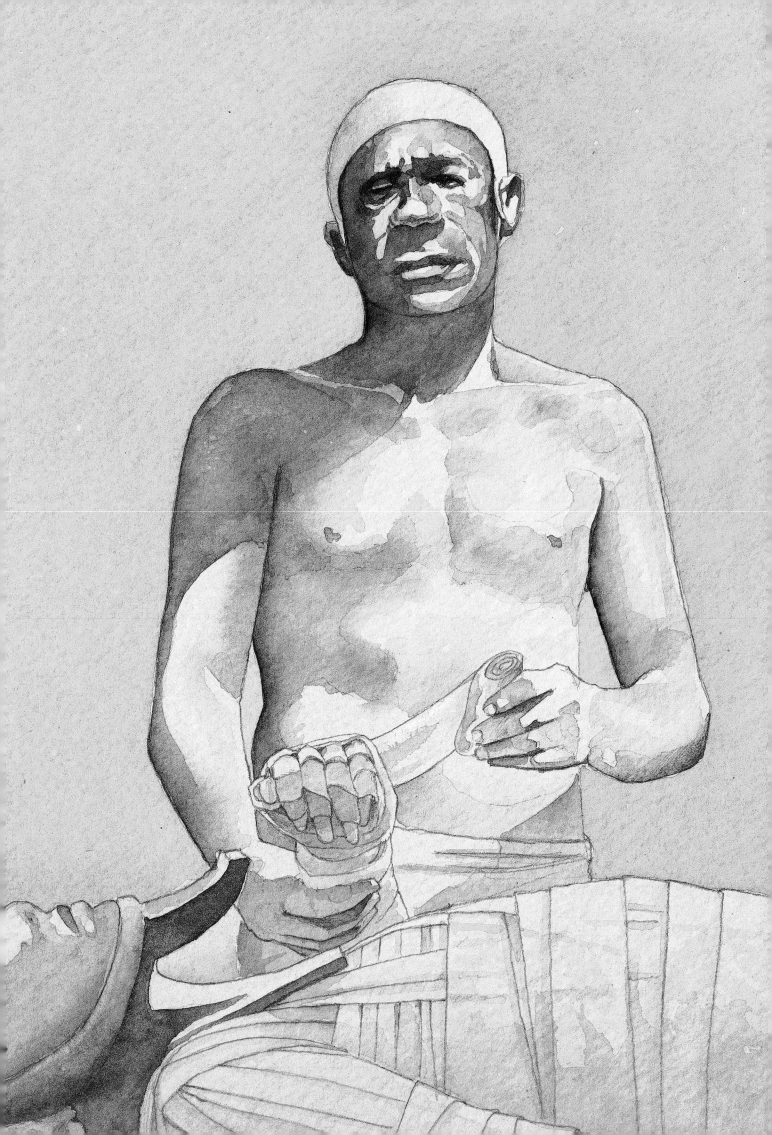

The Embalmer

"Come at once," the servant begs.

"My master is dead."

He is asking me, chief priest,

to perform the sacred rites.

Back at my workshop, I wash the body,

while another priest murmurs incantations.

My flint knife makes the first incision.

I take the stomach, lungs, intestines, liver

and store them in canopic jars.

I leave the heart, home of the spirit,

but pull the brains out with a hook of bronze.

We dry the body with crystals of natron.

Forty days pass.

We wind the head, the chest, the trunk, the limbs

with yards of linen.

On the eighty-ninth day

we place him in the cedar coffin.

Secretly, I believe the chief priests

are more important than Pharaoh.

No spirit can rise skyward without our sacred touch.

The Dancer

My troupe moves in and out as one,
no feast complete without our presence.

We dance to praise,
give thanks for the rising of the Nile,
the harvest gathered in.
We stretch and bend,
mirror one another in stately style.
We click our clappers.
The singers follow close behind.

We dance to mourn.
At the Feast of Eternity
we usher the spirit on his journey.
We celebrate the one who's gone
to the Field of Peace.
His statue watches.
Even when they are sorrowing,
we delight the guests.
I am a dancer.
My job is joy.

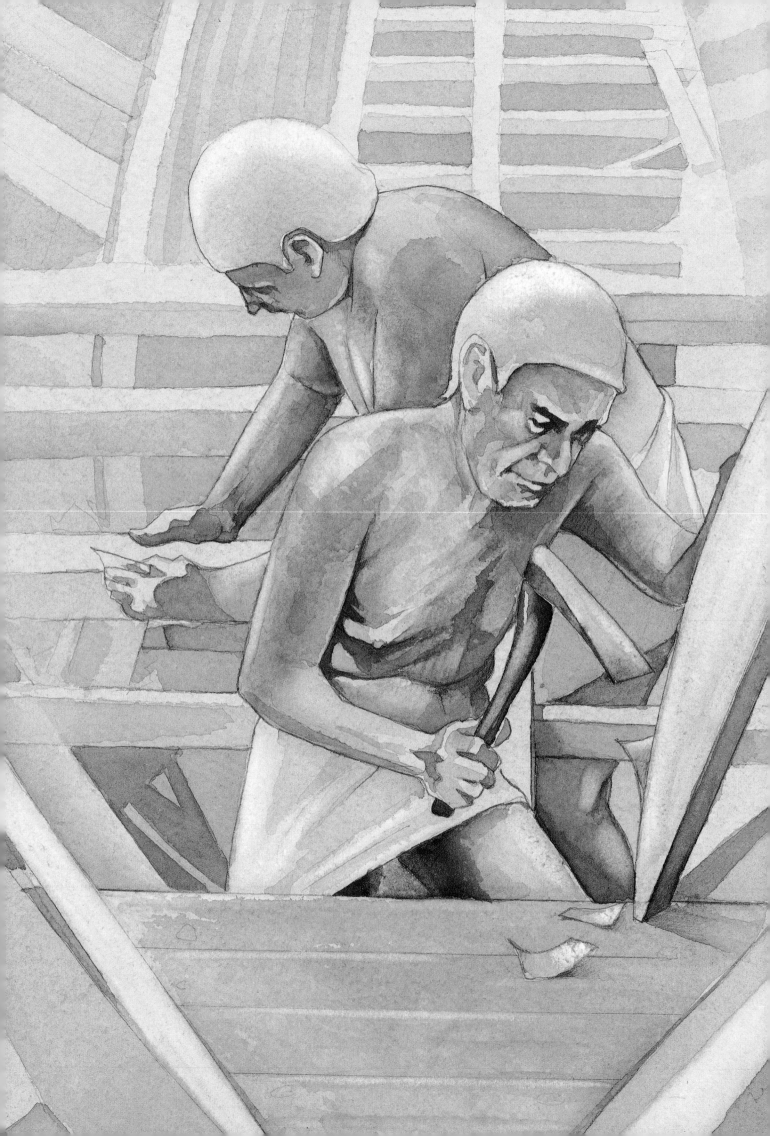

The Carpenter

The Pharaoh sends his carpenters to Lebanon

in search of cedar to build his barge.

I go with fellow shipwrights to the land of trees.

Wood is scarce in Egypt,

except the lowly sycamore,

too knotty to suit our careful craft.

We axe the trunks, cut the cedar planks,

and haul them home.

I use my adze, mallet, chisel, and saw

to shape the wood.

At last the ship is ready to set sail.

The Great One comes

and boards his barge.

He is well pleased.

I stand on shore and watch my weeks of work

afloat.

The Sailor

When I hoist the sails

like white wings of cranes,

off we go.

But when the wind weakens,

rowers dip and pull.

We sail south on the Red Sea

until the land of strangers can be seen.

After we dock, we lay out gifts—

beads, daggers, bread, meat, and fruit—

for the goddess Hathor.

Days pass while we fill our hold

with tribute for Egypt—

ebony, ivory, trees of myrrh,

and monkeys who climb and swing from the mast.

At last we travel home,

a ship of treasure from the place of Punt.

And I, a sailor, have been beyond.

The gods willing, I will go again.

The Marshman

Think of it!

A simple reed that grows in marshes

means Egypt's story will not be forgotten.

Papyrus lifts its feathery top high above our heads

as we labor in the wet.

We gather slim stalks and bind them into bundles.

Long and heavy, the load bends my back

but not my spirit.

We lift piles of plants so others

may build boats, twist rope, braid mats.

But best of all, papyrus

will be cut, pressed, dried,

transformed into paper!

Then scribes with watchful eyes

and ears so quick to listen

will record our messages,

our days, our dealings

for us to see,

and folk who follow after.

Historical Note

Ancient Egypt lasted for more than 5,000 years, beginning in the Predynastic period in 5200 B.C. and ending with the Roman conquest in 30 B.C. The foundation for much of the daily life, education, agriculture, craft development, travel, trade, religion, recreation, and funeral practices began during the Old Kingdom, approximately 2686-2160 B.C. and continued through the New Kingdom, which ended in approximately 1069 B.C. In this book I have tried to re-create the voices of people who might have lived, worked, played, and died during this time.

The Scribe: Scribes played a significant role in all periods of ancient Egyptian society. People of upper and lower classes depended on scribes to send messages, record events, register livestock. By the time of the New Kingdom the use of scribes had multiplied, and some recorders had specialized duties such as keeping the census, measuring the grain, and tracking military gains and losses. Scribes used a palette, water cup, and brush holder like those seen at the top of the scribe hieroglyph. In the picture, the palette, which contains red and black ink, hangs over the scribe's shoulder.

The Farmer: Agriculture was the major occupation of ancient Egyptians. Peasant families worked the fields, made fertile by the rise and fall of the Nile. Flax and grain were the major crops. After the sowing, herdsmen brought sheep and goats to trample the seed. During the harvest, a flutist sometimes played lively tunes to keep the workers moving. When at last the grain could be stored, a scribe tallied the results and calculated the state tax.

The Pyramid Builder: Pyramids were built from the Predynastic period through the Middle Kingdom. These "Houses of Eternity" were designed to keep the body of the Pharaoh safe so his spirit could make the journey to the afterlife. The workforce was made up of farmers, bakers, butchers, toolmakers, and others, all directed by scribes. These workmen were not slaves. They worked for Pharaoh during the flooding of the Nile instead of paying taxes or serving in the military.

The Herdsman: Herdsmen watched over their animals with great care. They talked to the cattle like children and gave them names. They lived with their herd and knew how to assist cows with calving. But in all three Kingdoms, Old, Middle, and New, herdsmen—unlike scribes or goldsmiths—were looked down upon by villagers as having a lowly occupation.

The Birdnetter: Birds were plentiful in ancient Egypt. Twice a year migrating waterbirds would stop to rest on the Nile after crossing the Sahara or the Mediterranean. In the Old Kingdom, clap nets like the one shown in the picture were used to trap huge catches of birds for eating. However, tomb paintings from the New Kingdom show that when noblemen and their families hunted for sport they often used a throw stick (like a boomerang) to stun the birds before capture.

The Washer of Clothes: Keeping clothes clean in a hot dusty land was not an easy task in any period in ancient Egypt. The chief washer was an important part of royal and noble households as early as the Old Kingdom. Middle Kingdom tombs depict washing and wringing. A watchful eye had to be kept for crocodiles lurking in the Nile where the washers worked.

The Weaver: Ancient Egyptians were well known for their exquisite weaving. During the Old Kingdom, women who served in households worked on horizontal looms. By the Middle Kingdom, the loom was a vertical one. Some cloth was taken to the treasury, which was called the House of Silver.

The Goldsmith: Even before the Old Kingdom, goldsmiths were skilled at beating, twisting, molding, and melting gold. Items such as bracelets, chokers, and hair ornaments were evident in pictures found in tombs of the Old Kingdom. Earrings did not appear until right before the New Kingdom. The development of fine jewelry making reached its peak during the New Kingdom. Goldsmiths used the semi-precious stones turquoise, lapis, carnelian, and amethyst to decorate their jewelry.

The Embalmer: Ancient Egyptians believed that to gain eternal life, the body needed to be preserved so the spirit could live on. In the early days of the Old Kingdom, limbs were wrapped in linen, but the body was left intact. Gradually priests discovered that bodies would not decay as quickly if organs were taken out. Embalmers began removing organs and placing them in canopic jars, containers used in funeral rituals. Removal of the brain began in the Old Kingdom, but was done on a more regular basis during the Middle and New Kingdoms. Crystals of natron, a salt, were used to dry the body. During the Middle and New Kingdoms, many bodies were stuffed with straw.

The Dancer: Music and dancing were part of every major event, whether it was the gathering of the harvest or the feast of Eternity for a departed loved one. During the Old Kingdom, the dances were stylized with only occasional acrobatics. The beat was set by clapping hands. By the time of the New Kingdom, dancers threw balls, beat on tambourines, clicked castanets, and did high jumps and complicated acrobatics.

The Carpenter: Lumber was in scarce supply in ancient Egypt. Finding the right wood to make coffins, boats, and furniture was difficult, even as far back as the Old Kingdom. A Pharaoh sometimes sent as many as 40 ships to Lebanon and Syria to bring back cedar and pine for coffins and boats. Shipwrights were extremely skilled at boat-building and could turn out a huge sailing ship in as little as 17 days. Boats provided the major means of hauling goods, materials, and passengers.

The Sailor: The Nile was the primary highway in ancient Egypt. Early boats were made of papyrus and were easy to guide. Wooden boats as big as 100 feet long and 50 feet across appeared in the Old Kingdom. The sailor looked after the sail and repeated the pilot's commands. The pilot used a speaking trumpet to call to men on shore. The land of Punt, thought to be located near present-day Somalia, was reached by sailing south on the Red Sea. Accounts of these expeditions do not refer to trade but rather to gifts to Hathor, the goddess of Punt, and tribute to Egypt from Punt.

The Marshman: The papyrus plant flourished in the Nile Valley during ancient Egyptian times and had many uses. Marshmen gathered the reeds and sent bundles of them to a workshop where they were used to make sandals, baskets, nets, and paper. Some reeds went to boatyards, where they were shaped into light boats. We owe much of our knowledge of ancient Egypt to papyrus scrolls that were preserved for thousands of years by Egypt's dry climate. The papyrus plant eventually died out in Egypt, but it has been recently reintroduced and is being harvested and processed.

Bibliography

Andreu, Guillemette. Translated by David Lorton. *Egypt in the Age of the Pyramids*. Ithaca, NY: Cornell University Press, 1997.

Billiard, Jules, editor. *Ancient Egypt: Discovering its Splendors*. Washington, DC: National Geographic Society, 1978.

Budge, E. A. Wallace. *The Dwellers on the Nile*. New York: Dover Publications, 1977.

Bunson, Margaret. *Encyclopedia of Ancient Egypt*. New York: Facts on File, 1991.

David, Rosalie. *Handbook to Life in Ancient Egypt*. New York: Oxford University Press, 1998.

Erman, Adolf. Translated by H. M. Tirard. *Life in Ancient Egypt*. New York: Dover Publications, 1971.

Hart, George. *Ancient Egypt*. New York: Knopf, 1990.

Malek, Jaromir. *In the Shadow of the Pyramids: Egypt During the Old Kingdom*. Norman, Oklahoma: University of Oklahoma Press, 1986.

Quirke, Stephen and Jeffrey Spencer, editors. *The British Museum Book of Ancient Egypt*. New York: Thames and Hudson, 1992.

Shaw, Ian, editor. *Oxford History of Ancient Egypt*. New York: Oxford University Press, 2000.

What Life Was Like on the Banks of the Nile: Egypt 3050—30 BC. Alexandria, VA: Time-Life Books, 1997.